EDEN HAZARD
The Wonder Boy

Copyright © 2019. All rights reserved to Sole Books.

No part of this book may be reproduced or transmitted in any form or by any means, electronic or mechanical, including photocopying, recording, or by any information storage or retrieval system, without written permission from Sole Books. For information regarding permission write to Sole Books, P.O. Box 10445, Beverly Hills, CA 90213.

To Lisa
A special thank you to Yonatan, Yaron and Guy Ginsberg.

Cover photo ©   ALTERPHOTOS/Manu R.B./
Sipa USA (Sipa via AP Images)

Design: Lazar Kackarovski

Proof editor: Louisa Jordan

Library of Congress Cataloging-in-Publication data available.

U.S. edition

ISBN: 978-1-938591-70-9

eBook ISBN: 978-1-938591-71-6

Published by Sole Books, Beverly Hills, California.

Printed in the United States of America

www.solebooks.com

Eden Hazard
The Wonder Boy

Michael Part

Read more in the Soccer Stars Series:

The Flea – The Amazing Story of Leo Messi

Cristiano Ronaldo - The Rise of a Winner

Neymar The Wizard

Mohamed Salah – The Egyptian King

Harry Kane - The Hurricane

Luis Suarez – A Striker's Story

Thomas Muller – The Smiling Champion

James – The Incredible Number 10

Balotelli – The Untold Story

Antoine Griezmann – The Kid Who Never Gave Up

www.solebooks.com

CHAPTER ONE
Belgian Fries at the Brussels Town Hall

The Brussels Town Hall overlooked the Grand Place in the middle of town, the aroma of the national delicacy, Belgian Fries, permeating everything. The returning national soccer team, known to those who loved them as The Red Devils, were ceremoniously served fries to celebrate their best showing in Belgium history at the 2018 World Cup. The aroma made everyone hungry.

The Town Hall was made of carved stone, several ornate floors high, and each floor, including the top floor, had a wide balcony that ran the entire width of the façade. The Red Devil squad was lined up just inside the hand-carved doors to the balcony, anxious to greet their fans below.

In the Grand Place below, hundreds of thousands of fans waited excitedly, dressed in red and waving their tri-color flags, hoping to catch a glimpse of their boys who had gone to Russia filled with hope, and returned home, heroes, having earned their beloved country 3rd place in the 2018 World Cup.

Roberto Martinez, the team manager, stopped next to Eden Hazard and grinned. "They are waiting for you."

"For us. All of us," Eden said.

Martinez nodded and stepped out onto the balcony. The cheers were deafening.

"When we were in Russia, we received many messages from you!" Martinez shouted into a microphone that broadcast all over the country. "Messages that said you believed we would make history. I hope we made you proud!"

The massive crowd below answered back: "WE ARE BELGIUM! WE ARE BELGIUM!"

Martinez turned and held the door open and Eden stepped out.

The crowd went nuts.

Next came keeper Thibaut Courtois. He'd kept the team in the World Cup with a series of spectacular saves against Brazil in the quarter-finals. He waved his arms around and the crowd answered back with a roar.

The rest of the team came out on the balcony, one by one, and received the love they had earned from their fellow countrymen.

Eden was moved by the adoration and fought back the tears as Romelu Lukaku draped his big arm over him. "It looks like all of Belgium is down there!" Eden said. Still, he looked like something was bothering him.

Martinez could see Eden wasn't 100% himself. "What's up, Eden?"

Eden couldn't believe he'd noticed. Was he being that obvious? "I just wish we'd gone all the way, coach," he said with a shrug. "That's it. I know, it's silly. I wanted to be a world champion."

Martinez knew Eden was always fighting for the number one spot. For his teams and for himself. Below, the crowd sang non-stop: "WE ARE BELGIUM! WE ARE BELGIUM! WE ARE BELGIUM!"

"You did your best and you made us proud," Martinez said, then moved on. Eden nodded, then listened to the shouting. It reminded him of the first time he'd heard this kind of chanting and singing. He was standing in his own backyard, in Braine-le-Comte.

He was just two years old. And this sound changed his life forever.

CHAPTER TWO
Beyond the Backyard Fence

Eden looked at the fence.

A ball flew over the wooden fence and landed near his feet.

Then came a deafening human roar.

The roar of the crowd, just beyond the backyard fence.

He carefully pushed some plants aside, revealing the hole in the fence.

The hole was on the bottom of the fence. It wasn't big, but he could go under it and crawl to the other side. He didn't do it. Not then. He just watched through the slats. The Hazard family backyard fence bordered with the local soccer club's pitch, Royal Stade Brainois. It was as if the pitch was part of their backyard.

The players drew near, their boots thumping, their bodies grunting. They fought each other like a herd of bulls chasing the ball.

Eden gripped the fence and watched as the two groups of men fought over the ball. He was so close to the action, he could see the sweat on one man's broad forehead, his longish hair wringing wet. The crowd on the other side of the fence, lining both sides of the field, cheered wildly.

One player, wearing the home team's white shirt, sent the ball to his friend.

Eden loved how they ran. He wanted to run with them. He cupped his hands on either side of his mouth and shouted. "Goal!"

In the next instant, the player kicked the ball into the goal and the crowd went crazy. He looked around and saw the little kid behind the fence hopping up and down. He made a face for the little boy, laughed, and charged off.

Eden giggled. That was awesome!

Later that day, Eden's mom pulled him across the living room and out the front door. She was strong because she was once a soccer player herself.

"Where are we going?" he asked.

"To the hospital," his mom said. "Your brother is about to arrive. But first we'll pick up dad."

She started the car and they peeled out of the driveway and headed up Avenue du Stade and disappeared around the corner.

His dad, Thierry, waited for them outside the Tivoli, the home stadium of La Louviere. Eden's dad was a professional player and he'd just finished training. He took over the wheel.

"When is the baby coming out?" Eden asked.

"Soon," his dad said.

"It's about time!" his mom announced.

"What's your favorite name for the baby?" Thierry asked his son.

"Thorgal," Eden said. He was his comic book hero.

Thierry laughed. "Well, I don't think we can name your brother Thorgal! When he grows up, people will expect too much of him!" He laughed some more.

Grandpa Francis and Grandma Nicole waited for them inside the hospital lobby and the whole Hazard family rushed into the elevator and his mom and dad entered the birthing rooms.

An hour later, Thierry came out. Grandma held Eden in her lap and Thierry took him in his arms and spun him around. "You have a brother," he whispered, holding his son with one arm and wiping some tears away with the other.

"Where's Thorgal?"

Thierry laughed again, a much-relaxed laugh. "We didn't exactly name him Thorgal, son, but we came close," Thierry said. "We named him Thorgan. After all, there's already a Thorgal."

That seemed to satisfy Eden.

That's when Eden heard his brother crying from inside the room.

The Wonder Boy

"That's Thorgan," Eden said. "He's here."

"He is indeed, son," Thierry said. "He's here, and he's hungry."

"When can we play soccer?" Eden asked.

He didn't understand why everyone laughed.

CHAPTER THREE
Mama Scores all the Goals

The small family house on Avenue du Stade in Braine-le-Comte was filled with soccer balls. They were everywhere and Carine, now pregnant again with her third son, had to weave through them to get to the kitchen. Everyone was already sitting around the breakfast table, waiting. Everyone but Thierry.

He wasn't missing for long. A few moments later, Thierry hopped into the kitchen on one foot, a piece of toast in his mouth, pulling on his La Louviere team shorts.

The rest of the family, grandma Nicole, grandpa Francis, four-year-old Eden, and two-year-old Thorgan, sat around the breakfast table watching him.

Thierry, snatched the toast from his mouth. "Sorry, I'm late," he said.

"You could ask for help," Carine said. "We are coming to watch you play and we would like you to survive long enough for your sons to see you.

Thierry flashed her a grin. "See you all in a bit." He tied the one shoe that was untied, grabbed his kit bag from its usual place, on the floor beneath the coat rack next to the back door, then hurried out of the kitchen. Seconds later, they heard the front door slam shut and he was gone.

When it was close to match time, Carine and Eden left Francis and Nicole behind to watch after baby Thorgan and headed over to the field.

They got the best seats. Eden wore his father's team colors: green and white, with "HAZARD" printed across the back.

Eden watched his father play intently. He was hopping up and down. "Goal! Goal! Goal!" he shouted.

"Why is daddy not scoring goals, mama?" Eden said, disappointed.

Carine grinned and hugged her four-year-old son. "Daddy's not a striker, honey, he's a defender." she said. "*I'm* the striker in the family. Mama scores all the goals," she added, laughing.

"I like goals," Eden said.

When everything was said and done, Thierry loped over to the stands to see his wife and son. "Did you enjoy the game?" he asked.

"Mama scores all the goals. Right, daddy?" Eden said.

Thierry burst out laughing and gave his wife one of his famous raised one-eyebrow looks. "Sure, she does, son. All by herself." He winked at Carine, then reached out his hands. "Come," he said and grabbed Eden from over the fence and took him in his arms. "Let's wave to the fans and thank them for coming."

"Yeah!" Eden shouted and as soon as his father set him down on the grass, he took off toward the circle to join the rest of his father's team. Thierry was next to him and they waved in unison to the cheering crowd.

"When I grow up, I'm gonna play here too," Eden said and his father smiled broadly. That was exactly his dream—to see his sons follow in his footsteps.

Thierry took his hand and they walked together across the grass to the changing room. When Thierry and Eden came into the changing room, all of Thierry's teammates greeted Eden and high-fived him and he loved it.

CHAPTER FOUR
The Hole in the Fence

There was a clubhouse at the end of the pitch, beyond the Hazard family fence. It had just been given a fresh coat of paint and the general manager of the Royal Stade property, Pascal Delmoitiez, walked out and came around the goal and took in a deep breath of fresh air. His plans today were to make his usual rounds, fix what needed fixing and clean what needed cleaning. He was a large, hefty man, with longish dark hair, mustache, and an infectious smile.

   He bent over and touched his toes. He knew if he could touch his toes, he could do anything. So, the first thing he did was scan the soccer pitch, expecting nothing special. Except, something small was moving in the distance, way at the other end of the field, near the opposite goal. He couldn't tell what it was. It had to be a living thing but it was too small to make out. Pascal thought about binoculars, which hung on a metal hook just inside the door to his office in the clubhouse. No. Why go back, he mused. He decided it would better just to move in for a closer look. Which he did.

When he moved downfield a little further, he could finally see that it was a small boy, not more than 5 years old. It was strange. He was barefoot.

The kid was shooting penalty kicks.

"Every, single, one of them in the top corner!" he exclaimed, then realized he'd said it out loud.

But how could a little kid like that shoot so well?

He knew he had to do something, but instead of chasing him off, he just stood there and stared.

Eden retrieved the ball from the net for the umpteenth time and when he turned, he saw the man in the distance, watching him. He knew he was the guy who chased kids off the field. He had seen him do it a bunch of times from the other side of the hole in his backyard fence.

That's when Pascal cupped his hands on either side of his mouth. "HEY YOU!!!" he shouted.

Eden's eyes grew wide. He snatched up his ball and ran for the fence.

Pascal cried out "No!"

He didn't want the boy to be hurt when he ran into the fence.

But the boy raced directly at the fence and instead of vaulting over it, he dove through it! It took Pascal a moment to realize there was a hole

The Wonder Boy

in the fence. The boy rolled in and disappeared inside.

So that was that. Case closed. Still, something gnawed at him. There was a reason he stayed on as the general manager of the grounds. It was his love of the beautiful game. And he also loved the job because of the thrill of finding new talent. He couldn't shake this boy from his mind. So, instead of marching off the field and going home, he marched off the field and walked down the road until he got to the front of the boy's house. He took a deep breath and stepped up to the front door and knocked.

Thierry answered the door and recognized Pascal instantly. "Pascal! To what do we owe this pleasure?"

Inside the house, Eden tried to sneak by in the background.

"Oh!" Pascal said. "Hello, young man!" he said to Eden.

Eden made a face and ran.

Pascal returned his attention to Thierry, who was now growing suspicious.

"Was that your son?"

"Yes, my oldest," Thierry said.

"Well, I'm here to talk about him," he said.

"Eden?"

"Yes," Pascal said, somewhat delighted. "Eden. I caught him on the field not half an hour ago and when I called out to him, he escaped into your garden. Your garden of Eden! I had just seeded the field and I'm afraid he made quite a mess."

Thierry raised an eyebrow. "I see. Excuse me a minute." He turned and shouted into the house. "EDEN!!!"

Eden appeared from the other room and skidded into Pascal's view across the hardwood floor. "Yes, daddy?" Eden said politely.

Thierry and Pascal both noticed Eden's feet were covered in mud. "I didn't notice that the backyard was muddy," Thierry said. "Pascal, did you just water the field?"

"As a matter of fact, I did, Mr. Hazard," Pascal replied. "After I seeded it."

Both men turned to Eden. "And you?" Thierry asked his son.

"I—I was on the field," Eden confessed, his heart beating fast.

Thierry studied Pascal, who smiled. "I know this breaks all your rules."

Eden kept quiet.

"To be honest, Mr. Hazard, I was going to invite him to train with our youth team and hopefully try out for our juniors." Pascal smiled. "It could be like a Hazard dynasty. Three generations."

Eden was confused. "Three?" he asked.

"Yes," Thierry said, counting them off on his fingers. "First, grandpa Francis, he was one of the founders of the club way back in 1969. Then I played for the club. And now you. If you make it."

Eden sucked in a breath.

"Every one of his shots went into the top corner," Pascal said. "It was a sight to behold. I don't know how he did it, he's only six, right?"

"Five," Thierry replied.

"Well! That's even more remarkable! And he did it barefoot!"

Thierry stared at his son with as much seriousness as he could muster. "Well now, Pascal. Asking my boy to join the team," he said turning to his son. "I suppose, that's as good a punishment as any."

The men burst out laughing.

Eden looked at them, confused. "Am I allowed to play on your pitch, sir?" he asked.

"I'd be happy to have you on our team," Pascal said.

Eden couldn't help it. He jumped up and down and screamed. "YES!"

CHAPTER FIVE
No Trespassing!

A week later, Eden entered Royal Stade Brainois through the club gate. He was summoned to the junior tryouts and was so focused that he never noticed who was watching him: Pascal, the man who recommended him to the team. He was also watched by club president, Alain Pauly. Both stood chatting on the touchline. Eden's father was in the stands, pretending not to bite his nails.

When Eden ran out on the field, he immediately joined the scrimmage in progress, led by Michael Pauly, Alain's son.

Pascal and Alain watched as Eden scrimmaged with the squad. After 10 minutes, Michael trotted over to his father, overflowing with excitement. "You see that kid?"

"Eden?"

"Yeah. Like father, like son!"

"Put him at the top of my list," Alain said and Michael wrote it down while Alain waved Eden over.

Eden saw the club president waving at him so he waved back.

The Wonder Boy

The club president waved some more and indicated he wanted him to come over. Eden sighed. He was having fun and didn't want to stop. The waving got more insistent so Eden finally turned away from the action and slow-walked over to the men. "Did you want to see me, sir?"

"Yes, I wanted to congratulate you. You're our newest club member," Alain replied.

Eden's eyes grew wide and he hopped up and down, too excited to stay still. "I got in? Thank you, sir!"

Pascal stepped up to Eden. "Tell the truth. What's more fun? Playing out there for the club, or getting chased by me?"

Eden giggled. "The club!" he said, then faked a few steps around the man and charged off, shouting over his shoulder: "You can't catch me!"

All the men laughed.

Eden rejoined the practice squad. He was where he wanted to be. A field. A ball. Boys to play against. Uniforms. Cleats. No more crawling under the fence and getting splinters in his butt. No more going barefoot to keep from getting his shoes muddy.

A little over two years later, Eden took the field as a seasoned 8-year-old Brainois star player and had already made a name for himself. Many of the spectators who filled the stands had come to see the genius they had heard about. They rooted for their sons, all right, but if pressed, most would admit to being fans of little Eden Hazard.

On a Sunday morning, just before dawn, Eden awakened with a start. Someone was watching him. He looked one way then the other and there was three-year-old Kylian standing on his side of the bed, unmoving. Silent.

"You promised," he whispered.

Eden sighed and looked around. It was just getting light. He got up and he and Kylian went and roused Thorgan and they all went out into the backyard.

"Now, you have to promise. What we are about to show you," Eden whispered," you have to promise to keep it a secret."

"I promise," Kylian said.

"Show him already," Thorgan said to Eden.

Eden nodded, stepped over to the fence, and moved a plant that looked like it was in the ground, but was really in a long, narrow metal container. He moved the plant revealing the hole under the fence. He looked over at Kylian. "Promise you won't tell anyone about this."

The Wonder Boy

Kylian's eyes were wide like full moons and he blinked nervously for a second. "P-promise!" he whispered, a little too loud.

"Shhhh," Eden warned and turned to Thorgan. "Let's go."

Thorgan nodded and hurried over and crawled through the hole and came out on the other side.

"Now you," Eden said to Kylian, who immediately scampered under and started to run down the field.

Eden crawled under the fence with one of his soccer balls and when all three brothers were on the field, Eden dropped the ball and kicked it to Thorgan and they passed to each other back and forth, keeping it away from Kylian, who started to cry until Eden lobbed it to him with a big smile.

After a few minutes, Kylian grew tired so the three brothers made the journey under the fence to their backyard.

"We're going to have to make sure no-one sneaks through when we're not looking, especially Kylian," Eden warned.

"Yeah, someone might kidnap him," Thorgan said.

"No!" Kylian shouted, terrified.

"Never leave him out here alone, at least until he is four," Eden said and turned to where Kylian once stood. "That all right with you, Kylian? Kylian?"

Kylian was gone.

"Hey!" Eden shouted and pointed through the fence. There was Kylian toddling through the grass on the other side of the fence, heading for the goal box. Both Eden and Thorgan realized what had happened and, one-by-one, dove through the hole to recapture their younger brother, and brought him back, giggling and covered in mud.

When Eden crawled back following his younger brothers, he saw two white slippers on the grass. His heart sunk. He knew who was wearing them and he knew what was coming.

His two brothers stood there frozen. He saw his mom's stern look. He stood up as fast as he could and tried to avoid her gaze.

"Whose idea was this?" she asked.

"Mine," Eden said.

"No, it was mine," Thorgan said.

"It was mine!" yelled Kylian.

Carine couldn't hold it anymore. She laughed out loud. The three boys were at first surprised, but they joined her laughter.

"I expected more from you, Eden," she said, then got serious again. "You're older. You should have known better."

The Wonder Boy

Eden expected to be punished. His heart raced in anticipation. He hoped his mom wouldn't ban him from playing.

"I'll never do it—ever again," he promised without waiting for his mom's verdict.

"I know you did it for your brothers." She turned her gaze to Thorgan. "I know you want to play like your older brother," she said.

"Yes, mom, I do! I want to play on a real pitch," he cried out.

"You'll get your shot," she said. "You'll play on a real pitch. Soon. Now get inside and clean yourselves up!" she ordered.

The next day, the hole under the fence was, once and for all, permanently filled in and a small wooden sign was posted, stating: "NO TRESPASSING."

CHAPTER SIX
THE SCOUT

The man in the stands watched Eden intently. He wrote these words furiously into his notebook: *The little skinny kid is fast. Great ball control. Has a vision. Dribbles a lot. A good finisher.*

The man, whose name was Fathi Ennabli, had begun secretly watching Eden as soon as he turned seven; now he was eight and the rumor about his playing had reached Fathi. People told him all the time about talented players, but he heard about young Hazard from several sources and was intrigued.

That's when Alain Pauly sat down next to him. "You're here more than you are with your own team, Fathi," Alain joked.

"I have no idea what you mean, Alain," Fathi quipped with a wink.

Fathi was the youth coordinator for Tubize, a second division team that played down the road. He had a 3-day-old beard, was of medium height, with short dark hair hidden under a red Tubize hat with a black bill. "Your boy is good, Alain."

On the field, Eden scored again and the people around Fathi and Alain all cheered loudly. Fathi leaned closer to one enthusiastic father. "Your son out there?"

The man laughed. "No, my son plays for the other team."

Fathi chuckled. "You mean, you're cheering for Brainois even though your son plays for the other team?"

The man nodded. "Yeah. The kids deserve it," he said.

"But, he's kind of a ball hog, don't you think?"

The father next to Fathi laughed. "If you're that good, why would you pass?"

Fathi returned to Brainois and found Thierry Hazard in the stands, watching Eden train. He sat down next to him. Thierry knew why he was there.

"Sorry, Fathi, Eden likes it here," Thierry said, then returned his attention to the match playing out on the field below. "It means everything to him."

"I know," Fathi said. "I'm just thinking ahead."

Thierry nodded, never taking his eyes off the match.

"You know as well as I that we can offer him so much more than he can get here at Brainois.

In case you forgot, I'm the one who signed *you* at Tubize."

"Fathi, you must know, you're not the first scout who has come to watch my son," Thierry said. "And I said no. He's too young."

Fathi stood up. "I'm not going to give up. I didn't give up on you, and I'm not going to give up on him. I'll keep trying, until I sign him."

Thierry smiled. He knew Fathi would be true to his word.

Thierry stuck his head in Eden's room. "Practice time."

Eden looked up from his book. "I want to skip it; would that be okay?"

Thierry studied his son. "You never miss practice. In fact, I usually have to drag you off the field." He thought about it for a moment. "Carine?!" He called for his wife and a moment later.

Carine stuck her head in the door.

"He wants to skip practice."

Carine looked her son over carefully. "What's wrong?"

"Nothing," Eden said. "I'm just bored. It's not fun anymore. I want to play with better players. I want to play against better teams. I want to learn from better coaches."

Carine and Thierry exchanged looks. Carine felt proud of her son.

Thierry nodded in agreement and smiled at his son.

Two years had passed since his "chance" meeting with Fathi in the stands. He knew what they had to do next.

"It's time to move," he said.

"Where?" Eden asked, his eyes shone with excitement.

"Tubize," Thierry replied.

CHAPTER SEVEN
A New Club

The Tubize pitch was a twenty-minute drive from Braine-le-Comte. Thierry parked the car in the adjoining lot.

Father and son got out of the car and made their way to the front office.

"This is the happiest day of my career," Fathi said quietly to Thierry as they entered his office.

"You said the same thing when you signed me," Thierry joked.

"Yeah, but I mean it this time." Fathi grinned.

The two men laughed.

Eden didn't have a clue what was so funny. He was excited and nervous. It was bigger than he thought. For a moment he felt he didn't belong. He followed his dad and Fathi outside to the training grounds where boys in yellow jerseys and red shorts stretched on the manicured pitch.

"Welcome to Tubize, Eden," Fathi said. He and Thierry stood on the touchline, talking.

"What do you think, son?" Thierry asked.

"I like it," Eden said.

Fathi waved at someone and a boy came over. "Show Eden where he'll be playing, Daniel."

The Wonder Boy

"Yes, sir," the boy named Daniel replied and turned to Eden. "Ready?"

Eden nodded excitedly.

Eden and Daniel charged off to join the boys in the center circle of the field in front of them.

Minutes later, Fathi looked up just as Eden raced by, the ball close to his foot. "That didn't take long," he said then turned back to the field. "Beautiful touch!"

Eden kept charging and Daniel moved into some space near the box, but instead of passing, Eden shot and hit the post. Daniel intercepted the bouncing ball but was covered by three players. He passed to Eden, who shot again and this time the ball flew into the upper left corner.

GOAL!

Eden hugged Daniel. "Thanks!" he said.

Daniel didn't look happy. "I passed. You didn't," he quipped.

Eden looked at Daniel and blushed. "I guess I didn't know if anybody else could do it."

"You have to trust your teammate. This is what they taught me here."

Eden nodded. "You're right," Eden said.

After practice, Eden walked off the field, surrounded by the other guys, all in a hurry to go home. Fathi stopped him at the door. "So, what do you think?" he asked.

"I like it here," Eden said.

"Great!" Fathi grinned. "See you next week."

Eden washed up then sat down at the dinner table next to his grandmother and grandfather, opposite his brothers. Eight-year-old Thorgan and six-year-old Kylian were already there, waiting for him, scowling. Eden looked from one to the other. "What? What'd I do?"

"You play for Tubize," Thorgan said.

"So what?" Thierry asked, scooping some potatoes on Thorgan's plate.

"It's not our team," Thorgan said.

"One day you'll be good enough to play with Tubize," his mother said.

"Let's go out back," Kylian whispered to Eden.

"Shhhh," Eden whispered back and Thorgan put his hand over his younger brother's mouth to quiet him.

With everyone served, Carine sat down next to her husband. "You don't look so good," she said to Eden.

"I'm tired," Eden replied.

Kylian never took his eyes off his oldest brother as he wolfed down his dinner.

Eden noticed and got the hint and hurriedly cleaned his plate.

The Wonder Boy

Kylian finished and leapt to his feet, grabbing a ball. "Let's go!" he said and raced out.

"Kylian!!" Carine yelled after him.

Eden and Thorgan shoveled the rest of their food into their mouths and got up and started to follow Kylian out.

"Hey wait!" she said. "I thought you were too tired!"

Eden grinned. "Yes but..."

She smiled. The love of the game was stronger than anything. She was like that at his age too. She understood what her son was feeling. He could play all day long. The desire to go out and play ball took over him.

"Hurry! We only have an hour of daylight left," Thorgan chimed in.

They all raced out to the backyard.

Inside the house, a half an hour later, Carine turned on the TV. It was almost time for their favorite soccer show.

She heard a rustling noise and looked up as Eden, Thorgan, and Kylian snuck past the doorway, trying to make it to safety in the other end of the house, making a beeline for the bathroom. All three were covered in mud.

"Stop!" she said and they froze.

She came over to the boys and squeezed some mud out of Kylian's ear, then looked at her oldest son.

Eden managed a smile. "Don't ask."

"I wouldn't think of it. Get cleaned up. All of you. It's almost time for *Téléfoot*!"

The boys all cheered at once and raced down the hall to the bathroom.

Thierry came into the living room and Carine chuckled. "Amazing how they won't listen to me, but they will listen to *Téléfoot*!" They both laughed and settled down on the sofa.

Minutes later, the entire family sat around the TV, glued to their favorite soccer program. The boys rough-housed and Carine and Thierry chatted, but Eden never took his eyes off the screen.

On TV, Zinedine Zidane lined up for a free kick and bent the ball around the wall and into the top corner of the goal.

Eden leaped to his feet. "Amazing!" He turned to his folks. "I want to play like Zizou."

"You need to work hard," his father said. "Very hard."

"I can do it," Eden insisted. "Exactly like him."

Thierry feigned a scowl. "It's good to have self-confidence, son. You obviously get that from me." Carine laughed.

On TV, Zidane headed in another goal. Everyone clapped.

I want to be like him, Eden thought. *And I will.*

CHAPTER EIGHT
Chess and Football

Eden made a run into the box. He passed two defenders but the third slammed into him. It was painful but Eden knew that he had something he'd always wanted—a free kick just outside the box. He'd trained for hours perfecting his free kick. He stood up slowly trying to forget the pain in his leg and focused on the kick.

His coach nodded. He wanted Eden to take it. This was their third league game and he saw his new player practicing free kicks after the training was over. He thought it was a good idea to give him an opportunity to show his skills.

Eden nodded back and placed the ball on the grass. He backed up, took a couple steps, and waited for the whistle. Then he breathed and looked at the wall they made of the other team's players. He looked at the keeper who was making himself ready by stretching his arms and yelling instructions to his defenders. Eden took three steps and shot. The ball curled around the wall and sailed into the top corner of the goal.

Everyone on the Tubize side of the stands were on their feet, celebrating!

The Wonder Boy

The ref blew his whistle and waved the goal off. "No goal! No goal!"

"What?!" Eden cried out.

The ref trotted over to him. "Next time, wait for my whistle."

Eden slouched right there on the field and kicked the grass. The ref was right. He hadn't waited for the ref to whistle because he wanted to take advantage of the unprepared defense.

He seemed downright calm as he saw his father in the corner of his eye. He took the ball and set it down exactly where it was before and this time calmly waited for the ref to blow the whistle.

Thierry turned to Fathi who was standing next to him. "I'd like to see him do *that* again."

Fathi chuckled. That kind of luck never happened.

The ref blew his whistle.

Eden shot again and the ball curled around the wall, *exactly as before* and it slammed into the upper corner. A perfect shot, not a millimeter different than the last.

"Wow," Thierry exclaimed, proud of his son.

Fathi smiled but his mood changed and he sighed. He knew it wouldn't be long before a bigger team would step in with an offer for his little diamond. He wondered how long he could enjoy Eden's talent. From the corner of his eye, Thierry saw Fathi's face and knew exactly what he was thinking.

He smiled.

The girl in the stands had long straight brown hair, and what caught his attention was not that she wasn't at all into the game played on the pitch, but rather, she was playing a game of chess with a friend who, like her, wasn't interested in the match.

While Eden ran his heart out on the pitch, the girl didn't even bother to look. Even the loud cheers from the crowd couldn't distract her and her friend from their own private, intense battle. Eden remembered seeing her at school but didn't know her. And she wasn't interested in the game, or him.

Who comes to a soccer match and plays chess in the stands? This doesn't make any sense!

When the ref blew his whistle and the soccer game was over, Eden scanned the stands for the girl, but she was gone. He rushed back through the clubhouse and instead of going straight to the changing room, he kept going, all the way out to the parking lot. He caught up with her and her friend as they were heading out.

"Hi," he said. "I'm Eden. Don't we go to the same school?"

She frowned at him as if he were a complete stranger. "Maybe, but I don't remember you, but I do play for the school team. Maybe you saw me playing."

"Do you come here often?" he asked.

She smiled. "I'm a fan."

How could you be a fan without even looking at the game, he wondered.

"My name is Natacha Van Honacker. I watched you out on the field. You seemed like you don't trust your teammates." With that, she spun and walked away with her friend.

"How could you watch me? You were too busy playing chess!" he shouted after them.

She stopped and turned back. She had a hard time keeping the smile back and stuffing a laugh. "Okay, so maybe off the field...you're a little nicer."

He came closer. "So maybe we can take in a movie sometime?" he said.

Natacha took a long time to answer. "Okay," she finally said and her friend rolled her eyes and pulled her along.

A week later, Eden and Natacha exited the movie theater. Thierry was waiting for him in the car.

"Cute girl. How did you meet her?" Thierry asked.

"At the match the other day," Eden replied. "She was playing chess during the match."

"Who won?" Thierry asked.

Eden grinned and leaned back in his seat. "I guess we both did," he said.

CHAPTER NINE
Enzo

Vincenzo "Enzo" Scifo watched the boys line up from the team office window. They were all waiting for him. He didn't want to mess this up. He was handsome and tall with short-cropped salt-and-pepper hair. He opened the door, like a curtain rising on a seasoned star, making his entrance, and trotted out to meet his players. No one said a word as he stood in front of them a short distance away. He studied the face of each boy before he spoke.

Scifo, now in his early fifties, was born in the same town where Eden was born and began his career at La Louviere, playing pro from 1982 to 2000. He was considered one of Belgium's greatest players ever and was nicknamed *little Pelé* when he played for Inter and Anderlecht.

It was 2002, and he was beginning his coaching career as Tubize's manager. His job wasn't just overseeing the first pro team. He was also put in charge of the youth teams.

He sensed the excitement of the young players seeing a star player standing and looking at them so closely. At his request, the players introduced themselves.

"Scifo scored four hundred and thirty-two goals as a junior player, can you believe it," Eden told his brothers before the training. He was eager to impress the new manager.

"Hello, boys," Scifo said.

The boys answered in unison. "Hello, coach."

Scifo didn't waste time. After each player introduced himself and had a short warmup, he split the team and watched them play.

A small kid caught his attention immediately.

"What's his name again?" he asked his assistant.

"Hazard. Eden Hazard. His two younger brothers are also playing here."

"He's phenomenal," Scifo said. He loved how Eden was handling the ball. His accurate passing and his finishing touch. The kid wasn't smiling much. He was immersed in the game. He worked hard and fought for each ball. Twenty minutes later, Scifo knew he was looking at the future of Belgium soccer.

"A bit arrogant. Thinks he knows better," the assistant said. "And he's not very strong, physically."

"That is exactly what they said about me when I was his age," Scifo said. "And I must tell you that I haven't seen a talent of this magnitude for a very long time."

The Wonder Boy

And then he quipped. "Let's enjoy him as long as he stays with us."

Eden led his Tubize squad out of the clubhouse and onto the field and saw, for the first time, something new in his field of vision: a line of men standing on the touchline with notepads, cell phones, and clipboards. Thorgan pulled alongside him and whispered: "Your fan club is here."

"They came for me?" Eden asked in dismay.

"You better believe it," Thorgan winked.

For Eden, it became a game within the game. Whenever he burst out of the clubhouse and out onto the field before a match, he would scan the crowd. Then he would make a game out of looking for scouts

"Don't tell me, Anderlecht again?" Eden said, almost bored, to his brothers, after the game. Anderlecht had been following him for a while, but he wasn't interested. He thought he was too good for them.

His brothers, however, thought otherwise. "Anderlecht is nothing to sneeze at, big brother," Thorgan said. "But it wasn't them this time. It was Jean-Michel Vandamme himself."

Eden was surprised. Surprised and pleased. "The Academy Director of Lille?"

"Yeah," Kylian said. "Although if you ask me, you don't deserve it."

"Yeah, well, I didn't ask," Eden said, irritated.

Thorgan gave Eden a look. "Kylian's right. So is Natacha. You need to get over yourself. You are too full of yourself!"

Eden loved sparring with his younger brothers, but he could also see they were serious and it embarrassed him. He had to admit, he did think of himself more than he thought of others, the exact opposite of what he was taught at home. No one said anything for a long while. Finally, Eden spoke up. "Is it really that obvious?"

Thorgan and Kylian nodded. "Plain as the nose on your face," Kylian said.

Now Eden was really embarrassed. He didn't like it when his own brothers pulled his covers. "All right," he said. "Thank you for being the best brothers in the world and for being honest." He hugged them, one at a time. "You mean the world to me."

CHAPTER TEN
Lille

Jean-Michel watched as Eden played. Both sides of the stands cheered him on. He was already a big deal. He was skinny and small, sure, then again, so was Franck Ribery, one of his discoveries when he first met him. He realized he would have to work hard to recruit Eden to Lille. He was still young and he'd have to leave home and live in France. But the boy was ready. Lille, in the north of France, just across the Belgium border, was an hour's drive from Tubize, so moving there wouldn't become an obstacle.

Jean-Michel scribbled in his notebook. He had already done his homework on Eden and knew what he would have to do when the time came. And he knew it was time. And he was aware of the interest other scouts showed in him. The clock was ticking. He had to move fast.

I got to get this boy! he thought.

After the match, he looked around until he found Thierry and cornered him for a chat.

"Mr. Hazard?" Jean-Michel said and stretched his hand for a shake.

Thierry stopped and turned to see who was hailing him. He recognized Jean-Michel immediately. "Off the top of my head I'm going to guess this is not about me moving to Lille," Thierry joked and Jean-Michel laughed.

"No, you had your chance, not that I don't think you could qualify, but I think it would look funny if I let you try out for our youth team. Let me be serious though, if I may. Your son has great potential," he said. "We would love for him to come play for us. I guess I don't have to tell you we have a strong academy and take really good care of our young recruits."

"His mother and I know all about Lille," Thierry replied.

"Then you also know he will need to move up to a stronger club soon. He's been here, what? Eighteen months?"

Thierry smiled. "You *have* done your homework."

"Well, I, didn't come here to see anybody else."

Thierry nodded. "It's a big move for Eden and for our family. Give us a couple days to think it over."

The two men shook hands again.

The Wonder Boy

The mood in the car when father and sons drove home was cheerful but serious. Thierry laid out the pros and cons for the move. Leaving home for Lille Academy wasn't an easy decision. But Thierry already knew the answer. And Eden knew that his parents and brothers would back him up all the way.

A couple weeks later, Eden said goodbye to Tubize and broke Fathi's heart.

"Remember us when you play for Belgium in the World Cup," Fathi said. Deep down inside he couldn't believe his best player ever was moving on so fast. He'd worked hard to bring him along and was as proud of him as if he were his own son.

The Hazard family came to Lille and took a tour. The grounds were vast, surrounded on four sides by brightly painted yellow buildings. Eden loved the feel of the place. As they walked, he whispered to Thorgan. "Don't forget our deal."

"Don't worry, I won't," Thorgan said with a wink.

Jean-Michel smiled at Eden when he was done showing them the grounds. "What do you think?" he asked.

Eden smiled. "I'm looking forward to playing here."

"Good," Jean-Michel said, ushering the whole family into his office. Once inside, Jean-Michel reached out and shook Eden's hand, then Carine's, then Thierry's.

"So, Eden, how do you see your future with us?" asked Jean-Michel

Eden flashed a grin. "When I'm sixteen, I'd love to be on the first team. I can't wait to play in front of huge crowds and blow their minds with my skills."

An awkward silence filled the room.

Thorgan cleared his throat. "Ahem."

That was the brother secret sign that Eden was being arrogant.

"I mean," Eden said fast, trying to correct himself, "I can't wait to play to win in front of all the Lille fans!" He looked over at Thorgan who nodded his approval.

Eden grinned and clasped his hands together. "Thank you for having me, sir. I won't let you down," he said and meant every word.

CHAPTER ELEVEN
To France and Beyond!

The whole Hazard family drove 14-year-old Eden to the academy. When they got there, Eden's new roommate, Jérémy, was there to greet them and show them the room. Eden looked around. Nice, but simple. Two beds, two desks, two coat racks, and two closets. One side of the room was already occupied by Jérémy.

"First time away from home," Eden whispered to Thorgan. He was nervous and a bit scared to be away his family.

Thorgan whispered, "I miss you already, bro."

Eden looked at his family. "I am going to miss you all."

"Well, what do you know," Carine said to Thierry but loud enough for Eden to hear. "Maybe he's growing up after all."

"Your mother and I are very proud of you," Thierry said to him.

"Is there anything you need?" Carine asked.

Eden thought about it. "No, I don't think so." Then he grinned. "Well, there is one thing."

"What's that?" Carine asked.

"A backyard," he said looking at his brothers. "With a hole in the fence. Where we all could play." He stretched out his arms. Kylian went first, followed by Thorgan, then Ethan, the youngest brother. Carine took Thierry's hand and together they watched their sons enjoy each other one last time as kids. She wiped a tear.

It finally came time for his family to return home and when they left, Eden stretched out on his bed. "Not as cozy as home, but not bad," he said out loud as Jérémy returned with a ball.

Jérémy smiled and flopped out on his bed on the other side of the room and tossed the ball up in the air, trying to get it as close as possible to the ceiling. After a minute he stopped and rolled over and propped up on an elbow. "How about a little kickabout?"

Eden grinned and just as he hopped out of his bed, Jérémy tossed him the ball.

"Let's see how good you really are," he said.

Eden intercepted the ball before it fell to the floor with his left. "You got it."

The boys went outside and played some one-on-one in the twilight and by the time they were done, Eden felt right at home.

Neither of them noticed the two men standing nearby watching them intently. Claude Puel, the

The Wonder Boy

manager of the first team, and Francois Vitali, the head of youth recruitment.

"Great skills but kinda slim," said Puel. "He has to get stronger.

"Yes," Vitali agreed. "He's going to need a lot of willpower."

The next day, the U16 coach, Stéphane Adam, marched across the field and took up a position in front of his team. He scanned the boys wordlessly for a few seconds. "Step up here, Eden," he finally said.

Eden took two steps forward and stood at attention.

"Boys, this is Eden Hazard. Let's congratulate him for joining our squad.

All the boys cheered the new kid. Eden stood there and thanked his new teammates. He knew that everyone around him was good, and everyone was thinking about their future as pro players. The competition would be fierce.

Bring it on, he thought when the first practice began.

A few months later, Eden was summoned to Vitali's office. He was asked to sit down and when he took his seat, he looked into Vitali's eyes trying to figure out why he was called to this one-on-one conversation.

"How do you like it here," asked Vitali.

"It's good," Eden said wondering where the conversation was heading.

"What do you think about your work here?"

"I think it's good," Eden said without flinching.

"Quite frankly, we think you don't do enough. We need you to work much harder. Day in and day out. We have a lot of talented young players here, and frankly, most of them aren't making it. You know why? Because they think talent is enough. But they are dead wrong. The best players in the game are hard working. And, they have talent."

Eden listened without a word.

"Now," Vitali said, "I took the liberty of inviting some special guests here today."

"Who?" Eden raised his eyebrows.

"I'll show you, come," said Vitali. They walked out to the adjoining room where his parents were seated with Mr. Vandamme.

Eden looked at his parents and sensed the gravity of the situation.

"Eden, we brought your folks here to discuss your future with us," Vandamme said. "Can you guess why?"

He wanted to crack a joke and say, *to tell them how great I am,* but he just said "No."

"Because we feel that you are missing out on an important opportunity you have here," Vandamme said.

Eden's heart sunk. He tried to avoid his dad's piercing look.

"We all believe in your great talents, but we also think you aren't putting in the hard work. You aren't trying hard enough, especially in your training. You only like to play games. You aren't interested in anything else. And you don't care enough about your schooling either."

Eden saw his mom's face toughen. She turned to him. "Eden, is all this true?"

Eden looked at his mom and said softly. "Yes, it's true."

The three men and his mom looked at each other. The way he said it was disarming. Carine tried not to smile. She was proud of her boy. He may have been lazy, but he was always honest.

"So, what are you going to do about it?" Thierry asked.

"I understand I have to work harder," Eden said. "So, I promise to do my best."

"I'll take you at your word," Vandamme said. The two Lille men left Eden with his parents in the room. They looked at each other for a long moment.

Eden nodded. "I'm sorry," he said.

"I trust you, son," his mom said. "I know you'll do the right thing."

"I won't let you down," he promised.

Eden was true to his word. He worked hard, constantly. He toughened up his body and spent many hours at the gym. As he got stronger, he got better. He knew that the hard work he put in was paying off. His coaches and parents were right.

In 2006, Eden was called up to the Belgium national U15 squad. He took a brief break from Lille and appeared in 5 matches for the national team and scored one goal before moving up to the U16, where he scored 2 goals in four appearances.

When his national spell was complete, he returned to Lille where he resumed working hard on developing his skills. His coaches admired him. They all agreed Eden Hazard had a bright future ahead of him.

When Eden moved up to the national U17 squad, he shared a row on the bus with teammate Christian Benteke. It was a special game for Eden and when the bus drew near, Eden pressed his face up against the window. The bus pulled into Stade Leburton, the Tubize home stadium Eden knew so well.

He looked at Christian with a smile. "I'm back home."

"Looks like you're gonna have to put on a show," Christian said. "Do you feel the pressure?"

"No," Eden said. He saw the smile of disbelief on his friend's face.

"Yes," he admitted and the two laughed.

The U17 squad was there for the European Championships. They were going up against the Netherlands. Eden wanted his family and friends to cheer him on. It was his first time back at Tubize in a couple years and everyone was in the stands.

Despite the fact that everyone Eden ever knew, including every member of his family, was seated in the stands, he only saw one person. He nudged Christian. "Do you see that double rainbow around that girl three rows up in the middle?"

Christian laughed. "Is that her?"

"Yeah," Eden said, and waved.

Natacha waved back. "She doesn't have her chess board with her," Eden said. "Which means she might actually watch us play."

By half time, the score was still 0-0, then in the second half, Eden was fouled.

Pascal Delmoitiez sat in the stands and watched with interest. He knew what came next: a penalty kick. And it brought back memories of him watching Eden the boy from afar as he shot barefooted one penalty kick after the other into the Braine-le-Comte goal.

Eden set the ball down. The Netherlands wall was formidable but he knew a way around it. He scanned the stands and saw his old friend Pascal standing. A little further down, he saw Natacha. He relaxed and took a deep breath. Then he took two steps and rocketed the ball into the upper left corner.

An overwhelming cheer erupted from the stands as teammate Omar Benzerga rushed him and hugged him and spun him around like a top. Later, the rest of the team engulfed him.

Belgium won 2-1 and went on to the semi-finals earning a third place in the European Championships, qualifying them for the 2007 FIFA U17 World Cup, to be held in Changwon, South Korea.

Eden waved to the cheering fans, especially to his friends and family, and took a deep breath as the sold-out crowd cheered like thunder.

He was going to South Korea!

CHAPTER TWELVE
Korean BBQ

The importance of playing in the Belgium U17 squad in the World Cup was obvious to the Hazard family. They'd discussed it before Eden packed for the trip. Eden would be playing before all the great teams and big clubs scouts from all over the world, a great opportunity to show his talent. In 2003, it was Cesc Fabregas and David Silva who made the journey that made them stars.

"Now it's my turn," Eden told his family just before boarding the flight to Korea. "To show who I am to the world."

The flight to Seoul took 13 hours and Eden slept through most of it. A number of formerly brave teammates were scared to death when they hit turbulence over Uzbekistan. The bus ride from Seoul to Changwon, however, was another story. At a distance of 200 miles, it should only have taken three hours, but it took four because the boys who weren't frightened by turbulence in the air, got car sick, and that included Eden.

The Belgium U17 squad was in Group E and on August 20, they charged out of the changing room after a rousing speech by coach

Bob Browaeys, to meet their opponent, Tunisia, as they headed for the tunnel in Changwon Stadium. Eden marched alongside Christian Benteke. "This is where we make the play of the day on *Téléfoot*!"

"I like the way you think," Christian replied.

They were all wearing red, yellow, and black. They marched through the tunnel and sounded like a herd of horses as their cleats echoed. It was 5 minutes to 5pm and music blasted from every PA system in Changwon Stadium.

When the ref blew the final whistle, the Belgians made their way to the changing room, their heads down. They'd lost to Tunisia, 2-4.

"I wasn't any good," Eden told his dad after the game.

"You were fine," Thierry told him. "But the team work has to improve."

"Not just that. It's me. I have to improve," Eden insisted. He knew he could do better.

Three days later, against Tajikistan, Eden led his squad to a 1-0 victory. Their next match would be in another three days, this time at Cheonan Stadium against the United States.

They lost 0-2 and went home to Belgium, bitterly disappointed.

Eden felt depressed. He knew there was a lot of talented players in Belgium and he wondered what it would take to be better. A lot better. Could his national team become a world leader?

Maybe one day, he thought, *and I want to be a part of it.*

CHAPTER THIRTEEN
Friendly Advice

When Eden returned to Lille, he knew he had to try harder. He was bothered by not scoring in Korea. He thought he had let his team down. One day, when he was coming off the pitch after a match, Stéphane and Claude Puel were waiting for him.

"How was Korea?" asked Puel. "How was it *for you*?"

"Well, sir, we didn't look good at all. And I–I didn't do so well myself."

"Well, I have to agree with you," Puel said. "But we can't look back. We need look forward, into the future."

Eden looked at the two men, dumbfounded.

"Eden, Mr. Puel needs someone behind the striker who can create plays," Stéphane said.

Eden felt his heart beat faster. "They want to move you up to the first team reserve for the upcoming season, and being on the bench could bring you faster than you think to the first team. While you do that, you'll also play with our U18."

"I hate to lose you," Stéphane said, "but we all know you are ready for a new challenge."

The Wonder Boy

"You looked a bit bored out there," Puel said.

Eden didn't say a word. He knew he could be much better with better players. The first team manager had somehow read his mind. Maybe they knew him better than he knew himself.

"Better players and much better opponents will make you a complete player. It will force you to improve. To work harder. It is a great opportunity for you and I believe you can do it, even though you are only sixteen," Puel added. "And of course, we are going to sign you up for your first contract. We'll send an offer to your parents. But I think they should first hear this from you." The man smiled.

Eden shook Puel's hand and Stéphane's hand. "Thank you, I won't let you down."

He went to the changing room, pulled out his phone, and told the news to his parents.

"Wow," Thierry said. He wasn't totally surprised. He knew it was coming. Still, he didn't think it would happen so fast.

"You make sure you step up to the challenge," Carine said to her eldest son. "Show them your true colors!"

"I will, mom," Eden said and went looking for his brothers. He wanted badly to break the news to them. When they saw his broad smile, they knew it was something good. The Hazard brothers had a way of speaking to each other with very few words. They were as happy as he was when he broke the news.

"This is sooo exciting," Kylian said.

"I knew it was coming," Thorgan yelled.

They hugged. Eden realized, at that moment, that his loving soccer family was the best thing that had ever happened to him. He didn't stop smiling for the rest of the day.

His first team appearance came on November 16, 2007, when Eden made his first-team debut against Club Bruges. He came in as a sub and impressed the coach who, a week later, included him on the roster for his first League 1 game against Nancy, one of Lille's major rivals.

When Eden stormed on the field for the warm-ups, he saw his entire family and Natacha sitting in the stands. He wore the red and white number 33 Lille shirt. Although he didn't start, he felt proud and elated.

Nancy had just scored their second goal at the 77th minute when Eden was called a minute later to sub for Fauvergue. Sixteen-year-old Eden Hazard's official professional career had begun. The Hazard family in the stands were on their feet, screaming his name.

Eden worked hard, but the score didn't change and his first game ended with a loss. Nonetheless, he was happy. He knew there were many games ahead of him. When the final whistle blew, he closed his eyes for a moment and concentrated on how much fun he'd had.

Puel patted his back. "You did great, son," he said.

CHAPTER FOURTEEN
Eden Goes to the Mountain

Patrick Kluivert, the Dutch striker, came over to Lille from PSV in 2007. In his storied career, he had scored over 130 goals for Ajax, AC Milan, and Barcelona and was only sidelined when injuries slowed him down. He was tall, over six feet, of Cameroon descent, born in Amsterdam.

He stood in the box and kicked the ball into the goal post so he could return it. *If I'm not that old*, he thought, *why does everything hurt?*

He bent down to pick up the ball. That's when he saw someone watching him from the touchline. Eden. He knew him and he knew what he wanted, so he waved him over.

Eden took a deep breath then jogged over to the box where Patrick was practicing. "Hey, Patrick," he said.

"How's it going, kid?"

"Well, to tell you the truth, I've been kinda slacking off lately, when it comes to training."

"So I noticed," Patrick replied and kicked the ball again. Top post. Return. Kick goal. "Look, Eden, you're doing the opposite of what you're supposed to be doing now that you're a senior.

The Wonder Boy

You need to work harder, not less. You gotta give more than a hundred percent. The team needs you to make those plays. You make those plays by training and practicing, not by biting your nails waiting to be called in. You need to work so hard that there's no doubt you've earned your place on the squad. That's what it is like to be the best. I know you have it in you."

He turned to the ball. "Left side post," he said nonchalantly, then kicked. The ball slammed into the left side post and returned. He chased it and side-kicked it into the net. Then he turned and flashed a grin at Eden.

"Nice," Eden said. "And thanks."

On his seventeenth birthday, Eden made a vow. "This year, I become a regular starter for Lille," he said and blew out the candles.

"From your mouth to God's ear," Carine said and cut him a thick slice of cake. Thierry was next, then Kylian, then Thorgan, then Ethan.

Thorgan toasted his big brother. "To the soon-to-be best player at Lille!"

Everyone toasted. Eden smiled. "Not so fast," he said. He knew he had to work really hard to earn the praise. And in his heart, he vowed to make it happen.

The new Lille manager, Rudi Garcia, threw the number 26 jersey to Eden. "It's yours. You deserve it."

Eden caught the new jersey and quickly took off his old number 33 and pulled on the new one. He looked down at the new number and admired it. Then he looked up at his mates. "How do I look?" he asked.

"Like you're moving up in the world," said Mathieu Debuchy.

"You look like seven less than 33," Yohane Cabaye joked with a smirk. Everyone laughed.

Eden was grateful for what Patrick Kluivert had shared with him and those around him thought highly of him, but all of them had one thing to say: great talent isn't enough and without the right attitude and hard work, his newly launched career will go nowhere. For Eden, all he wanted was an opportunity to show how good he was and how serious he was about the future.

In September, Eden got his chance to be something more than just a lazy braggart.

Lille was down 2-1 against Auxerre. Rudi Garcia turned to the bench. "Eden! Get ready! You are coming in."

Eden got up and took a deep breath, remembering not to hold it. He shook the fantasy of scoring a goal out of his head. This was about

The Wonder Boy

team work, not glory. *It was about winning, not me*, he thought.

He was busy, into the game, chasing the ball, making tackles, focusing on the right passes. What happened next, he would remember forever. The ball sailed right to him, near the penalty box. It was like everyone from both teams were in the box and there was no room to pass to anyone. So, he made a swift decision to shoot. The ball went into the back of the net, just like it belonged there.

He couldn't believe it. He'd scored his first goal ever for the first team!

He turned just in time to be hit by a wave of his fellow players, who piled on top of him.

Then, in stoppage time, Tulio de Melo scored the winning goal for Lille.

In the changing room, Rudi Garcia, standing in the middle, summed up the game for his players. "Tulio scored the winning goal, but Eden's goal was the turning point in the game. I was just told that Eden is the youngest goal-scorer in Lille's history. Give him a hand!"

Everyone clapped and cheered. "Eden, Eden!"

Later that evening, the sports media in France was talking about the new 16-year-old that was making history. Eden loved every minute of it. He was the happiest person on earth.

Two months later, in November, Eden got his first professional league start. Saint-Etienne were formidable opponents. Eden was aware of the opportunity he got and he vowed to seize it.

Twenty-five minutes in, he got the ball and showed some fancy footwork that completely confused his defender while Eden bent the ball cleanly inside the goal rattling the net.

That night, Eden's goal was shown on *Téléfoot*.

And the next day, Rudi Garcia made him a permanent starter on the senior team.

CHAPTER FIFTEEN
Tuxedo Junction

"Today, as all of you know, is our final league match. It's a must win or we don't qualify for the Europa League. If we win, we're in. Now let's get out there and make some great plays!" Rudi Garcia finished his talk in the changing room.

The team clapped in unison and charged out, making a lot of noise. Rudi liked it. It got his blood pumping.

The final match was against their arch nemesis, Nancy. It was a sold-out crowd in Stade Pierre-Mauroy and they were waving their red and white flags and cheering frantically. Everyone in the stadium knew that they had to win.

Lille scored first with Eden's assist and by minute fourteen, Lille was up 2-0, but Nancy fought back and scored their own two goals. A score of 2-2 was not good enough for Lille. A draw wouldn't move them on to the Europa League. They needed a win, or it was all over.

With only fifteen minutes left, Eden set up a third goal and helped his team pull into the lead, which they held until the joyous end. Eden was the hero of the match and Yohan lifted him high into the air. Lille got their 5th place in the league and, for them, it was a glorious victory.

That season, Eden played 35 matches and scored 6 goals and lots of assists.

He became the Lille fans' favorite. The entire league talked about him. Everyone said he had a bright future ahead of him.

The French national team scout, Claude, came to see him at Lille and caught up with him coming off the pitch. He introduced himself and told him he wanted to bring him to play with the French. "We have no one like you, Eden, you would be our star striker. We would love to have you join us. You're already here at Lille, that must make you half-French already." All Eden had to do, he argued, is get French citizenship. The man told him basically that there was no future for him with the Belgium national team. In other words, the Belgians would never be a worthwhile contender in the European Championships or the World Cup.

They just weren't good enough, was the French scout's message.

Eden smiled politely. "I'm sorry, sir." He chose his words carefully. "But I am a proud citizen of Belgium," he said, and the two parted ways.

A week later, Eden showed up at the Belgian national training camp and an old friend was there to greet him.

The Wonder Boy

"Kevin!" Eden said and hugged his old Lille team mate, winger Kevin Mirallas. He had just moved from Lille to Saint-Étienne.

"About time!" Kevin said. "I thought you'd never get here! We're going to give Luxembourg plenty of grief!"

On November 19, 2008, Eden took the field in the 67th minute at Josy Barthel Stadium in Luxembourg for the first time as a Belgium national, substituting for forward Wesley Sonck. Eden's mate Kevin Mirallas had scored first in the 22nd and Luxembourg's midfielder Mario Mutsch equalized the score at 1-1 in the 46th. The score stayed locked at 1-1.

Then Eden came in. The minute he took the field, all 4,172 spectators were on their feet. It didn't matter which side Eden Hazard was on, they were happy to see him.

The November friendly was also the 100th anniversary match for Luxembourg, so he gave them an anniversary present. Within seconds, he took over the ball and immediately looked around for Kevin. He saw him out of the corner of his eye across the field, matching his pace, running down the touchline, so Eden zigzagged downfield, matching Kevin's speed, keeping the ball away from the defenders, tricking them with his footwork, heading straight for the box. He got some space and looked over. Kevin was marked. No good.

Eden quickly took one touch and shot.

And missed.

The match ended in a draw, but for Eden it was a first and he felt good about it. He knew there were many more games for him in the future with the national team.

As he came off the field, team captain Daniel Van Buyten was there to greet him and slapped his back. "Congratulations! You're the seventh youngest international player!"

While Eden changed, his teammates all came over to congratulate him on his international debut. The last to visit him was his coach, René Vandereycken. "Before you go, I just wanted to let you know you're one of four players on the list for the Ligue 1 Young Player of Year."

An avalanche of feelings ran through Eden's head in that instant. *The Ligue 1 Young Player of the Year. Zinedine Zidane won it. Thierry Henry won it. Now it's my turn*, he thought.

"Don't let it go to your head," René said, breaking Eden's reverie. "You haven't won it yet."

Eden snapped out of it and grinned. "You know me too well, coach."

René nodded. "Where you off to?"

"Somewhere I can stop thinking about myself."

The Wonder Boy

René laughed as Eden ran off to break the news to his parents and brothers.

In May, Eden pulled on a scratchy, ill-fitting tuxedo and with Natacha on his arm, went to the Ligue 1 Awards.

Natacha covered her mouth so Eden wouldn't see she was giggling. She sat beside him in the long sedan sent for them to bring them to the biggest annual awards program in France.

Natacha shook and took Eden out of his nervousness. "What are you laughing at?"

"You," she giggled. "That suit. You look very elegant but very uncomfortable."

Eden smiled. "Beyond belief," he said.

That night, Eden won the award for Ligue 1 Young Player of the Year. He was the first international player to win the French award.

When he went off stage, he felt that everything that was happening to him was beyond belief because it had happened so fast.

He was only 18.

CHAPTER SIXTEEN
Praise from a Hero

Eden, racket in hand, whacked the ping pong ball as hard as he could and twisted his wrist. The ball corkscrewed over the net and curved into the right-hand corner, sailing off the table and slamming into the wall behind Gervinho.

Eden's phone buzzed in his pocket and he set the paddle down. "Hold on," he said and answered the phone. It was Thorgan.

"Did you hear the news?!" Thorgan said.

"Don't tell me. You're going pro?"

"No! I mean, yes, but that's not it. Zinedine Zidane just mentioned you in an interview!"

Eden's eyes widened and he stood frozen behind the table.

Gervinho looked at him, worried. "You okay, mate?"

Eden looked at Gervinho and nodded, then looked at the phone, then put it back to his ear. "What did he say?"

"Here, let me read it to you: 'Hazard will be a major star in the future'. I'm sending you the link."

Eden dropped the paddle and stood still. "I can't believe it," he muttered.

The Wonder Boy

"Can't believe what?" Gervinho asked.

Eden didn't say another word, he just bolted outside to get some privacy. He clicked the link Gervinho sent him and the Zizou interview popped up on his screen. He read it, mouthing every word Zizou had said out loud. "Eden is technically gifted and very fast."

When he told Natacha, she was thrilled. "You know Zidane is an adviser to the President of Real Madrid. Maybe they want you there?"

"I wish!" Eden said. It has always been his dream to play for Real.

He needed to talk to his parents so he drove home. At the door, Carine answered and grabbed him and hugged him. "So glad to see you! But why are you here? Is something wrong?"

Eden chuckled. "No, nothing's wrong. I just want to talk with you guys. I need some advice."

Thierry smiled when he saw his son. "Good to see you," he said.

"It's all Zizou's fault," Eden joked.

Thierry looked his oldest son over. "I saw the interview. You must be up on cloud nine!"

"Yeah, but that's not why I'm here."

"Aw, you're here to see your mom and pop, that's so sweet," Thierry said and winked.

"That's also true, dad, but it's not the only reason," he said. "I need to talk to you."

Thierry sat up straight. "Oh! Of course! What's on your mind, son?"

"People are talking about all the teams who are looking at me. They're all wondering where I'll sign next season."

Thierry smiled. "You should stay with Lille one more season. There is no need to rush these things. If you stay, you'll be more prepared for such a big move in a year."

"I agree," Carine said. "You're still young. You'll get better offers and you shouldn't rush."

Eden smiled. "You're right. This is the year Lille should win the Europa League."

"All the more reason, son," Thierry said. "They can't do it without you."

Eden smiled and hugged his father. "Thanks."

CHAPTER SEVENTEEN
Two Time's the Charm

Eden couldn't sleep the night before the match against Liverpool. The practice that day was grueling. When he got to the field, they had a meeting in the changing room. Rio Mavuba, the team captain, stood on the bench so everyone could see him. "Listen, guys. Yes, they have some great players! Steven Gerrard, Pepe Reina, and Fernando Torres. But we have Eden Hazard!"

Everyone in the room cheered.

Now Eden realized what his mate from the squad national, Christian Benteke, meant when he said he was glad he wasn't him because of all the pressure. He felt it now. He took a deep breath. His father was right. The team needed him and for the first time in his life, he felt nervous. Responsible. He didn't want to let anyone down.

Right from the start, Eden felt the pressure. Liverpool's defenders were on him like a swarm of bees. They were fouling and making it hard on him to find empty spaces for himself, and do what he was good at, dribble and find a free channel for passing.

Eden Hazard

Eden saw Rudi at the touchline, cupping his hands on either side of his mouth, shouting. He knew what he was shouting to him. When you have three defenders all over you, there is a vacancy on the other side. Try to find an open winger at the other side of the pitch. But it was tough. And the clock was ticking.

With five minutes to go, Lille won a free kick.

Eden lined up for the shot, took a few steps back, and bent the ball over the wall of Liverpool players and it made a quick bounce and shot all the way back into the left-hand corner. GOAL!

The stadium exploded. Now they just had to keep the net clean for the rest of the match, which they did. Lille took the match, 1-0.

A few weeks later, Eden sat in the most comfortable chair in his agent John Bico's office and watched him as he came around from behind his desk and sat on a corner for his usual talk. "They're all after you! Barcelona, Real Madrid, Arsenal, Chelsea, Inter Milan, you name it. You're a star! They all want to sign you for big money. The big question is, who do you like?"

Eden's heart beat out of his chest. He wanted to race around the office on the walls, he had so much pent up energy right then, so he breathed deep and pretended he didn't care. Finally, he decided to speak: "You know me, John. I like Real Madrid and Arsenal."

Bico grinned. "You're so predictable. Your heroes, Thierry Henry and Zidane are there. Of course. You know, the French awards are coming up soon."

"Yeah, I know," Eden replied.

"Young Player of the Year again," Bico said. "That's never happened before."

"Should be fun," Eden said and shifted in his chair. He wanted to leave.

"This time get a tux that fits."

Eden laughed.

"I'll do my best, just for you," promised Bico.

A couple weeks later, Eden and Natacha stepped out of their limo in front of the French Footballer of the Year Awards ceremony.

An hour later, Eden won Young Player of the Year for the second year in a row. A first.

When they finally got around to announcing the Player of the Year Award, Natacha squeezed his hand.

"Lisandro Lopez of Lyon!" the announcer said over the PA system.

Natacha frowned and looked over at Eden. He was fine. "Hey, we were fourth in the league," he said. "We'll just have to do better next year!"

She kissed his cheek.

"We'll get it next year—when we win the league!"

Natacha hugged him tight. "That's what I love about you. Always the optimist."

Eden smiled. It was a time to celebrate.

The following week, it all fell apart.

CHAPTER EIGHTEEN
An Attitude of Gratitude

From the day he won the award, nothing went right for Eden. He couldn't score. He had no energy. Negativity took its toll. It unnerved him.

It unnerved everybody. Especially Rudi Garcia.

"I'm moving you to the bench," Rudi told him and waited for Eden to respond, but he didn't. He'd seen that look before. He was depressed. "You're just not doing well enough to start, but don't let it freak you out. It's just a slump. Everyone has them."

"Even me?" Eden tried to smile. He was down. He was exhausted.

"Even you," Rudi said. "Try not to let it get to you. You'll be back."

Easy for you to say, Eden thought. He had been trying to stay positive, but it was not easy.

Natacha got on the phone with Thorgan. "He won't leave the bedroom," she said.

"You gotta get him out of there," Thorgan replied.

Eden came to the bedroom door when Natacha knocked lightly. "I want to help," she said.

"I don't need it," Eden replied. "I don't know what's going on," he said and slammed the door in her face. He turned from the door and plopped face-down on the bed. He wanted to cry but he couldn't. He heard the click of the doorknob and knew Natacha had come in.

"You don't know what's going on?" she asked. "Well, I do. You're not perfect. And you're back to thinking you are. Everything else is going fine. This is just a bad moment in a good time."

He rolled over. "A lot of bad moments," he said.

"They're going to need you," she said.

He shook his head. "They're doing fine without me. Gervinho and the new guy, Moussa Sow, are kicking butt out there. They don't need me."

She looked down at him and knew what he was going through. "I know what this is. You're feeling sorry for yourself. You're on the pity pot."

That stopped him. He knew she was right and he couldn't think of anything to say.

"You got everything going for you, Eden." She turned and left the room.

A few moments later, there was another knock at the door. Eden thought it was Natacha and opened it. It was his teammate Yohan. "Let's play some FIFA!" he said and came in. "How's it going?" he asked, eyeballing his friend.

"Fine. Great," Eden replied.

Yohan didn't buy it. "I don't think so," he said.

"Nothing you can do about it."

"No, but I've been there. You need to relax, bro. This will pass. Besides, the Euro 2012 is coming," he said, waving his game controller around. "We need to practice!"

Eden laughed and they went into the living room.

A week later, George Leekens, the new coach of the Belgian national team, stood eye-to-eye, toe-to-toe with Eden, in his office. "I don't like your attitude," he said. "I'm not even going to put you on the bench."

Eden felt desperate. "What'd I do?"

"It's what you *didn't* do. You didn't work hard. You slacked off. What happened to you?"

Eden sighed. He knew the coach was right. He nodded and left the office.

His father was out in the stands, waiting for him. Eden went over and sat down next to him. "I guess I am lazy. Zizou says those nice things about me and I think I can skate. But dad, you know, I *hate* training."

Thierry riveted his son with a glare. "So what?"

"Come on, you know I can do this."

"Sure, I know. And you know. But your coaches—they don't know. That's why you gotta prove it to them, out on the pitch."

"When?"

"When do you think? Every day! It's not just for you, Eden. You gotta do it for your family too. This is what you wanted to do. Get back to that time when you couldn't wait to sneak under the fence, you loved the game so much."

Eden bit his lip, and hugged his father. "What would I do without you?"

Thierry looked at his son and hugged him tighter. "I love you, son."

In a match against Azerbaijan, he came on, created some plays, and helped the national team. After the game, the team assistant manager Wilmots told him "There, that wasn't so bad."

"So why don't you start me?"

"Because it's not just about your talent, Eden."

"Okay, now I'm confused," Eden said. "I think I need your help."

Wilmots studied him. It was times like these that he remembered he was dealing with a 19-year-old kid. "All right. First thing is, you gotta be consistent. You know, back in France, at Lille, all they talk about is your fancy footwork and your goals, but they never mention that you aren't a team player. You're too much focused on yourself. Focus on being a part of a machine. A machine that can't run without you."

Eden thanked Wilmots. He knew he had to talk with Rudi.

"I have to admit, I've been feeling sorry for myself. Natacha thinks I should be grateful."

"She's right," Rudi chimed in. "You should be grateful for what you got. My papa used to tell me, any time I started feeling sorry for myself, that I needed an attitude of gratitude. So, get out there on the pitch and give it your all. I may not know what it's like to be a two-time winner of the Young Player of the Year, but I know what it's like to be nineteen. We can do this together, Eden. But you gotta listen to me."

"I will," Eden promised.

Eden kept his promise and turned it around one more time. He cranked it up on the pitch and inspired the team for the next five league matches. When it came to free kicks, he always came through.

In the fifth match, he took yet again a free kick, and won the match for Lille.

The crowd went wild.

From the depths of despair, Eden rose to great heights in the weeks running up to the end of the season.

And to top it all, Natacha and Eden welcomed to the world a newborn baby. They named him Yannis.

CHAPTER NINETEEN
Two Finals

Eden took a deep breath. The pitch at Stade de France felt like a country unto itself. Their host was Paris Saint-Germain and the stands were filled with their cheering fans. It was Eden's first final ever. And It was Lille's first cup final since 1955.

His nerves were raw. This final was a showstopper of great magnitude in his and his teammates' collective minds. But as the game progressed, the two sides couldn't find the back of the net.

Two minutes left on the clock and the score was 0-0.

The referee whistled for a Lille free kick. It was Eden's territory. But not this time. It was a perfect shot for a left footer. He signaled to Ludovic Obraniak. "Your shot," Eden told him and he nodded.

Ludovic took the shot and Eden could have sworn he saw it in slow motion. It floated over the keeper's head and into the net.

GOAL!!

Ludovic froze, stunned for a second. When it sunk in, and he heard the crowd, he unfroze as a group of his mates headed his way. He ran ahead of them and slid along the grass as Eden caught up to him and jumped on top of him like he was a surfboard and they skidded to a stop in front of the adoring crowd.

The final whistle blew.

Lille had won the 2011 French Cup.

But there was no relaxing. They still had the league title to win.

Their opponent was, again, Paris Saint-Germain and they needed only one point to win the title. The match ended in a 2-2 draw. It was enough.

The entire Lille squad celebrated and lined up in front of the fans and bounced up and down applauding them.

Eden scanned the stands as they bounced and found Natacha and his son Yannis, a few rows back.

He climbed up and picked her up and danced with her in the seats, surrounded by his adoring fans.

Two weeks later, it was announced he was up for the Ligue 1 Player of the Year again. It didn't matter to him. What mattered was Natacha and his son. His family. And his team. And he would do anything for them.

When his name was announced as the winner, he didn't even hear it at first. The tux fit perfectly this time. Natacha nudged him back to reality and he went up on stage and received the award. He faced the crowd and closed his eyes for a moment. He knew he hadn't done this alone. He looked around the crowd in the dark and knew his entire family was out there. So were his coaches and teammates. He was grateful for every painful moment that had led him to this stage.

He was the youngest Ligue 1 Player of the Year in history.

CHAPTER TWENTY
Goodbye, Lille

Eden took his father's advice and stayed one more season at Lille. Lille gave him the number 10 jersey and put him behind the striker again, exactly where he had always wanted to be, ever since he was a kid.

The Zizou space.

He had just turned 21 and all his dreams were wrapped up in playing for a club that was playing regularly in the Champions League with teams like Barcelona or Real Madrid. Before the last match of Eden's final season in Lille, he'd already scored 19 goals.

Now he got ready for his last game with Lille against Nancy, their archrival.

The night before the game, he tried to picture the future. He settled on thinking about the game. What could he do to leave a mark? He wanted to make his last game count for the club who had taken him in when he was 16 and, in just five years, made him a star; a player who was coveted by big clubs. He wanted to turn the last game into a gift for the fans. A lasting memory. And he knew he was going to give it everything on the pitch.

The Wonder Boy

The next day, Rudi waited for him in the changing room and handed him the captain's armband. "I'm going to miss you. A lot," he said.

Eden nodded and slipped on the armband. "Thanks, coach."

"Looks good on you. I have a feeling about today. A good feeling."

"Me too, coach. I'm gonna make this one unforgettable."

"For us?" Rudi kidded.

"Yes, for the team, the fans," Eden replied and winked. "And for Nancy."

Rudi laughed and Eden joined in. He stuck out his hand and Rudi shook it and Eden pulled him in for a hug. "This one's for you, coach."

Rudi nodded. He was already missing Eden Hazard.

The Stade Pierre-Mauroy was overflowing with fans. Most wanted to bid their favorite player goodbye. Eden tried not to think about it on the field. Minutes later, he ran the ball down field and chipped it over the goalkeeper's head and it slammed into the net. There was number 20. He had made his goal and it was easy. He felt as if he was gliding on a wave of grace and goodwill.

The crowd cried out for "more!"

Eden did it again. He moved fast across the back of the box and totally fooled the keeper and kicked the ball lightly in. He quickly ran into the roaring crowd and flashed two fingers.

A few minutes later, Lille won a penalty. Eden felt the inevitability of it all. The crowd cheered and sang and drowned out all other noise.

The goalkeeper dove left and Eden lobbed the ball into the right-hand bottom corner. He had gotten his first-ever hat trick in the perfect game at the perfect time.

The game ended. He felt elation and sadness. His time with Lille was over and it was hard fighting back the tears after they won the match. It was time. He stepped up to the microphone to say a few words. The fans stayed in their seats, waiting for this moment, cheering wildly.

"Thank you so much!" he said and took a deep breath. "I will miss you all!"

As the crowd cheered, Eden took one last look at the stadium and his team.

It was like saying farewell to his youth. He came here young and hopeful. He was leaving on a high note as a man. The fans, his teammates, his family. Everyone wished him luck. He was always confident. Some might say arrogant. But now when he looked at the fans, tears choking in his throat, he hoped he was ready for what the future had in store for him.

CHAPTER TWENTY-ONE
Hello, Chelsea

When the offer came from Chelsea, Eden's reaction was a huge surprise. It wasn't his first choice. But the offer came, and Chelsea was a world powerhouse and he knew that the Premier League was considered by many to be the most competitive in the world.

Chelsea scout Guy Hillion had been watching Eden for a while. He loved the fact that Eden could play on the wings, behind the striker, and he could take on defenders with his dribbling skills, make perfect passes, and score. He had vision, touch, and he was agile and fast.

And so, by 2012, Eden Hazard became Chelsea's number 1 prospect, ever since Roberto Di Matteo took over as manager in March of that same year. They were 5th in the Premier League and 20 points behind Manchester United. They were also in danger of missing a place in the Champions League next season. They had plenty of money, but no superstar to lead them out of the doldrums.

"Okay," John Bico, Eden's agent said when they met to discuss his future. "I assume you've done some soul searching?"

Eden shrugged. "I guess you could call it that. It's kind of hard to forget where you put your lifelong dream. I already told you my first choices are Arsenal or Real Madrid."

Bico smiled. "Okay, so here's how it is. We want at least 30 million Euro and both of those clubs are balking. The teams that are ready to open their purses are Man U and Chelsea. "Di Matteo called earlier. He wants to talk to you in person. You are going to London to meet him."

"When?"

"Now. They are sending the owner jet to pick you up."

An hour later, Eden had lunch with Chelsea's manager, Roberto di Matteo in a fancy restaurant in London.

"We want take the lead in the Premiership and Europe," the manager said and explained to him how he saw his contribution to the team before concluding with "We see you as our new star in the making."

Eden smiled. "Thank you, coach. I'll think about it."

On the way home, Eden got a call from Roman Abramovich, the owner of Chelsea. When he got home, he told Natacha "We're going sailing over the weekend."

"Sailing?" she looked at him surprised.

"With Chelsea's owner. On his yacht."
"They really want you," she said.
He nodded, smiling.

The Eclipse was over 533 feet long, the second largest private yacht in the world, worth over $1.5 billion.

Both of them lounged on Deck 8 with some other guests, sipping fruit juice and getting a tan. They got the royal treatment, especially Eden. If he got too hot, there was a pool just a few yards away, while 5 of the 92 crew members catered to his every need. While he rested, another helicopter besides the one that brought him out, came in and landed on the topmost deck, Deck 9. If he got hungry, food was brought up from the Deck 6. The cabins and suites were on Deck 3.

He felt like a king.

Half an hour later, Eden was in the elevator going down to the dining hall with his host. "We want Chelsea to get to the highest level, Eden, and I already know we can't do it without a creative playmaker like you. The fans will love you."

Eden's heart raced. He was impressed but also knew deep down inside that this was about playing, not yachting. "Do I have to give you an answer now?"

"No, of course not," the owner said. "You don't answer to me anyway. That's why I have a manager. I just wanted to make sure there was no doubt in your mind how much I personally want you on our team."

"I appreciate that, sir," Eden said. "I'll think about it."

The owner smiled. He knew he was looking at the future of his team. "That's exactly what I want you to do. I want you to know deep down in your heart that you can play in the blue shirt at Stamford Bridge for years to come."

A couple days later, his phone rang. It was his old friend and teammate, Gervinho, who had signed with Arsenal the year before. "I know what you want. You want me to come to Arsenal."

"Not at all," Gervinho replied. "I have someone here who wants to speak with you."

It was Didier Drogba, one of the best strikers in the world and Chelsea's hero. He introduced himself and after Eden caught his breath, he spoke. "I hear Chelsea made an offer and you're on the fence about it."

"That's right," Eden replied.

"Well, fences have holes."

Eden burst out laughing.

"Did I say something funny?"

"No," Eden said. "It's just a private joke between my childhood and myself."

"Well, my point is, fences can be gone through. I just wanted to tell you that signing with Chelsea was the best decision I ever made. I've been here eight years. Eight fantastic years. Come join us! It's a great club and the fans are amazing. This is where you can become an international superstar."

"I'll think about it," Eden said. "Thank you."

He knew what he had to do: talk to his father.

"I want a team I can lead to the trophies," he told Thierry.

"I know. It's gotta be hard making a decision when you're torn between what you have always wanted and who wants you. The decision is yours and yours alone, son," Thierry said. "Remember though. They sound desperate to sign you. That is a very good thing."

"You know me, dad, I want to play every game. It sounds like that is where it will happen. My one worry is, they're down so far, they might not make it into the Champions League next season."

"So, you wait for the end of the season," Thierry said. "You wait for a sign."

Chelsea finished 6th in the Premier League that season. But they made it all the way to the Champions League finals against Bayern Munich. If they won that match, they would be in next year's competition in spite of their Premier League standing. Eden wanted them to win because he wanted to take part in the Champions League in his first year with Chelsea.

Eden watched the match with his brothers from the best seats in his house. Despite all that, his nerves were a jangle. It turned out to be a tense but fairly mediocre game. Thomas Muller finally scored in the 83rd minute for Bayern.

Just then, Chelsea equalized the score. Didier Drogba, the man who had urged Eden to join Chelsea, just tied the match with a powerful header. Eden leaped out of his seat.

The match went into overtime and penalties. Didier Drogba was the last of Chelsea's five. If he scored, they win the Champions League.

Didier stepped up and pulled a fast one. He sent the goalkeeper diving the wrong way, then calmly dropped the ball into the goal, scoring the winning goal.

Chelsea won the sought-after trophy at last.

Eden felt elated. He knew what he was about to do.

The Wonder Boy

A week later, Eden sent a tweet to his millions of followers. It was a simple tweet: *I'm signing for the Champion's League winner.*

CHAPTER TWENTY-TWO
A Shy Proposal

Eden's debut in the Premier League was against Wigan FC.

Ten minutes into the game, he set up his first goal and won a penalty for the second.

When he came off for the half, Roberto was there to hug him. "Eden, you totally blow my mind," he said.

With 30 minutes left, Di Matteo sent in a substitute for Eden and, as he trotted off the field, he got a standing ovation from the Chelsea fans.

After the match, a reporter stuck a microphone in his face. "So, what do you think of the Premier League? You look tired, by the way. Is it tougher playing here than in France?"

"It's not the physical effort, it's the intensity. There's no time to breathe! The Premier League is 100% all the time!"

The reporter continued. "So, what are your plans?"

"To get used to it." Eden laughed and jogged off.

The Wonder Boy

A week later, Eden scored his first Premier League goal for Chelsea in a match against Newcastle at home. There were over 40,000 fans in the stands to witness it. He calmly and deliberately struck it. Right in the bottom corner. With that, Eden Hazard entered the Chelsea history books.

Natacha met him as he stepped out of the changing room as the boys trotted off. "We're going to have a baby," she whispered in his ear. Eden closed his eyes. It was a rush. He couldn't think of better news.

At dinner, that night, Eden reached across the table and took her hands. "You're my best friend," he said. "We have been together since we were fifteen…"

"Fourteen," she interrupted.

Eden chuckled. "Time flies when you're having fun. Listen, this is hard for me."

"Right, yeah, the shy thing," she said.

"You're a great mother and a fantastic friend. There is no way I could do this without you," he said. "Will you marry me?"

Natacha smiled that smile that had reeled him in all those years ago. She said yes.

Chelsea wasn't doing well and Di Matteo put Eden in as a defensive midfielder to shore up the squad. Eden hated it.

Juan Mata knew how Eden felt but he brought him up to speed. "Look, mate," he said, "Chelsea paid you a ton of cash. I even saw it on the news. They paid you to play in whatever position the boss wants you to play, so get with the program!"

Eden knew Mata so instead of listening to his own head, he took Mata's direction.

But things didn't get better for him. A month later, in a match with Swansea, the ball boy fell on the ball in the middle of a play.

Eden saw him and rushed over to him and kicked the ball out from under him.

The ball boy angrily leapt to his feet. "He kicked me in the ribs!" he yelled to the ref.

The ref answered by yanking out a red card.

That was it. He had lost it. Eden looked at his feet and marched off in shame. Frank Lampard matched step with him on the way off. "I know you were just trying to get the ball from that troll. Don't worry. You are freaking out defenders everywhere we play. And that's a good thing!"

Eden thanked his teammate, and left the field, a little less in pain.

CHAPTER TWENTY-THREE
Mourinho

Chelsea's home field, Stamford Bridge, known as *The Bridge*, was full to the brim the day Jose Mourinho came back to town. Mourinho stood in front of the Chelsea squad and observed them without comment. Satisfied, he decided to speak. "Anyone need an introduction?"

All the players shared the laugh. When the laughter died down, he continued. "I've been here before. And now I'm back. And I have big plans for you. All of you."

"How does it feel?" someone asked.

Mourinho grinned. "I'm back because I love this club. Last year, you won the Europa League and came very, very close to winning the FA and League Cups. I'm here to get us over the hump. In other words, I'm here to take you all the way." He smiled.

Eden smiled and Mourinho noticed. "Something wrong, Eden?"

"Well, boss," Eden said. "I heard that you are very self-assured."

Mourinho laughed and everyone joined in.

"I'm not known for my modesty and neither are you," he quipped and everyone laughed again. "I'm laughing now, but I won't be if you don't work your tails off. All of you. We're not going to get there by buying more expensive players. We're going to get there by working hard for the team. Not for ourselves." With that he stared directly at Eden.

A few minutes later, after his talk, Mourinho had a one-on-one with Eden. "I have big plans for you. All you have to do is listen and be a team player. You can do great things. You can earn a place in the world soccer stage like Messi and Ronaldo."

"Thank you, boss," Eden replied. He had heard it before but it was great to hear it from one of the best managers in the world.

"Boss, I was wondering about something."

"Go ahead," Mourinho said.

"About Willian and Andre," Eden replied. He was talking about the two new players Chelsea had just signed. Willian from Brazil and Andre Schürrle from Germany. Both number 10s.

"What about them?" Mourinho said. "If you play well, the number 10 is yours." With that, he walked away, then turned back after a few steps. "I know you will," he added.

Eden flashed a grin. "Thank you, sir!"

The Wonder Boy

A week later, Eden overslept and missed the training. When he finally showed up, he was given a message to report straight to Mourinho.

"Why did you skip training?" the new manager asked.

"I trained yesterday. I feel great!" Eden replied.

Mourinho beckoned him over with a wag of his finger. "I want you to see something."

Eden stepped up and Mourinho showed him the team roster on his clipboard. He took a pen and scratched Eden's name off the list. His eyes met his star player. Eden was clearly upset. "The correct answer, when I ask you why you skipped training, is *no excuse, sir*. If that is too difficult for you, you will have plenty of time to practice saying it, while you're on the bench." Mourinho shrugged. "That's all."

The next game, Eden scowled. Mourinho kept his promise and confined him to the team bench.

Out on the field, Chelsea was winning without him. He watched Willian and Andre both play in his position behind the striker.

After the game, the two met for a talk. "I hope you know I'm trying to help you here."

"I do," Eden said. "I guess."

Mourinho locked eyes with him. "Your problem is, you're like the boxer who keeps getting in the ring. He gets in the ring, he gets beat up and tossed out. Instead of learning to stay out of the ring and saving himself a lot of pain and suffering, he gets back in!"

Eden listened intently.

"We already know you don't like to train, but skipping it—it's time for you to figure out it's not working for you. You gotta stop getting in the ring, Eden. You don't like to train? Too bad. You're gonna do it, or I'm gonna knock you back out again. Think about it. And be ready for our next match. You can make it up to us then." He walked away.

Eden had to admit, he did feel beat up. He also knew the great Mourinho was right.

Mourinho kept his word and put him back in a match against Sunderland. He had never felt as much team spirit as he did that day. It was like the sun was shining down on him. Unfortunately, the weather wasn't as cooperative. It poured down rain and everything was soaking wet.

Minutes in, Eden dribbled into the box and crossed it to Lampard who headed it into the net. Frank ran over and kissed him on the forehead. "What a ball!"

Twenty minutes later, Eden got the ball and ran it down the left side where he came up against the Sunderland defense. He saw his teammate, Cesar Azpilicueta, on the other side and faked sending the ball to him, then instead, raced to the penalty area and zipped a shot straight into the goal.

The fans went mad with joy. Eden looked over at the touchline. Mourinho was watching with the biggest smile he had ever seen on his face. In fact, because it was so rare, he pointed at it. In the second half, Eden scored another and when the match was over, Mourinho hugged him. "Your best performance yet!" he exclaimed.

Eden left the field elated. His teammates and coaches all had faith in him again and more importantly, he had faith in himself.

In 2014, Eden went to Brazil and played for Belgium in the World Cup, along with a number of his Belgian friends. His teammate, Christian Benteke, couldn't play due to injuries, so he and Romelu Lukaku had to pick up the slack. Although he did not score a single goal, he got a taste of the intensity of the World Cup, and knew in his heart he would be ready for it in 2018.

CHAPTER TWENTY–FOUR
A Team Effort

The thousands of fans in the streets of Brussels below where Eden stood all sang together and drowned out all sound. WE ARE BELGIUM! WE ARE BELGIUM! WE ARE BELGIUM! Looking back on everything that had got him here, Eden knew what it took before Courtois could ask.

Thibaut Courtois came back over to Eden's side after national team manager Roberto Martinez left and took in the adoration from the crowds alongside his teammate. Natacha came out on the balcony shepherding their three sons: Yannis, Sammy, and Leo. She kissed his cheek. "You look relaxed," she said.

Eden smiled. "Been doing some thinking."

"Uh-oh," Courtois said. "That could be dangerous."

Natacha laughed. Their three sons surrounded their father, just as he and his brothers had surrounded their father when they were young.

"Okay, I'll bite. Thinking about what?" Natacha asked.

Eden looked over and smiled. "Believe it or not, I was thinking about the fence."

"The fence?" Courtois asked.

"There was this fence that separated my backyard from the soccer field. It had a hole under it. And that's how we all got out to play on a real field. It was a long time ago, but it feels like yesterday."

"So, it was a fence that got you here," Courtois said.

Eden chuckled and shook his head. "No, it wasn't a fence. It was a team effort."

Courtois chuckled. "I could've told you that."

Eden nodded and hugged his family. "I know. I'm just grateful I figured it out for myself."

CHAPTER TWENTY–FIVE
A Goodbye and a New Beginning

Eden's 2018–19 season for Chelsea ended on a high note, winning the Europa League—beating their archrivals, Arsenal, 4-1. His two goals and assist ensured that the final would forever be known as *his* final. Everyone in the stadium in Baku, the fans at home, and the world of soccer, knew that this might be his last game at Chelsea.

As a farewell, it could hardly have been more spectacular. "I think it's a goodbye," he said within minutes of the final whistle when he was asked by a reporter what his plans were. "Maybe it's time for a new challenge." He was already thinking about his hero. He knew he was closer to fulfil his childhood dream. He was happy for Chelsea's win. And he was excited to start again.

He was thinking about how Zinedine Zidane had left his coaching job at Real Madrid before the last season had begun. He needed a break. He left a winner and a club that was at its peak. But the news of his departure unnerved Eden. More than anything, especially after seven seasons leading Chelsea to a second Europa League cup, Eden wanted to play for Real Madrid under Zizou. When Zizou became the first-team coach, he put in motion a plan to bring Eden Hazard to Real Madrid, recommending him, just like he did all those years ago in 2010. As the 2018–19 turned out a disastrous season for Real Madrid and after two managers were fired, Zidane was called back to save the club and he agreed to step in. He returned to helm the team again in the middle of the season but his eyes were set on the next season, hiring new players and building an energized squad that will bring the club the three coveted trophies: La Liga, The Spanish Cup, and the biggest trophy of all, The Champions League. And he knew who would fill the void Cristiano Ronaldo had left. This was meant to be. Perfect timing for both men.

Eden pulled on his boots in the Bernabéu changing room, after having dressed in the Real Madrid all-white kit. He couldn't wait to stand in front of the 50,000 fans who stood in line to get in to cheer for their new star player. His family was there and the fact that he now wore the Real kit would not be lost on them: it had been a lifelong dream. He remembered when he and his brothers and his mom and dad had sat around the TV, glued to their favorite soccer program—Zizou had lined up for a free kick and bent the ball around the wall and into the top corner of the goal and Eden had leapt to his feet in his living room, declaring his goal in life to play like Zizou.

This time when he jumped up, he was instantly surrounded by reporters. "Rumor is," one reporter came forward, "you've always wanted to play for Real Madrid."

Eden's heart leaped. He grinned. "I have dreamt of this moment since I was very young, since I was playing in my family's garden," he said. "And now I have just signed a five-year contract with Mr. Perez." He looked across the Real Madrid locker room where Florentino Pérez, the club president, stood. It had been a long time since he felt this happy. He nodded at Eden. It was almost time to introduce him to the world as a Real Madrid player.

The reporters left and Zizou appeared from out of nowhere and sat down on the bench across from Eden. "I was looking forward to this day," Zizou said. "You look good."

"Me too. Oh, and thanks for those kind things you said about me."

"Can I confess something?" Zizou asked.

"Of course," Eden replied.

"I know you said many times it was always your dream to play for Real…"

"Yes! But to play for you. Not just for Real. For you."

Zizou grinned. "Well, I just want you to know, there's no one else in the world I want on my team more than you."

Eden fought back the tears and thrust out his hand. Zizou took it and together they gripped so hard Eden swore to his father later that night, that they could have forged diamonds.

"Come on," Zizou said. "Florentino's waiting. I want to introduce you to your fans." He draped his arm over Eden's shoulder, and they walked out the tunnel together.

The roar from the crowd was deafening. It felt like coming home.

THE WORLDS #1 BEST-SELLING SOCCER SERIES!

www.ingramcontent.com/pod-product-compliance
Lightning Source LLC
Chambersburg PA
CBHW031406040426
42444CB00005B/433